AYANA FAROOQ

WHERE WILDFLOWERS BLOOM

To Nana, for writing to publishers and showing my poems to all his friends. And to his friend Arshad uncle for reading every early poem draft.

CONTENTS

Dedication
ii

1 — Predator
1

2 — Prey
11

3 — The Grounds
31

4 — The Hunt
42

PREDATOR

WHERE WILDFLOWERS BLOOM

I had nothing but a bow
And the tall grass
The sky was all orange hues

I glimpsed horns
Antlers that were about to grow

But you hid them well
Convinced everyone you were as innocent as a deer

I waited

As you dashed around
Evading me

I would spend my life hunting you
It gave me purpose
I would kill you
And then I struck
While I saw you one morning
Grazing between two trees

But as I pierced your heart
Mine broke too

I stared at your fallen body
Purple wildflowers clung to your skin

Left to wonder
Was I the real beast?

AYANA FAROOQ

It seems like the more you stab me in the back
The wider the path is from my heart to you
You give me so little
Just enough
To caress the shadows of your love
The ghost of a smile
The tickle of your touch

WHERE WILDFLOWERS BLOOM

I should've called you Marco Polo
One foot on shore
The other in the sea
One hand enveloped in mine
The other out exploring
One eye gazing into my soul
The other sailing to her lips
Your body sleeping next to me
While your heart lies with her

I thought I could take some scissors
Bright red markers
Purple Elmer's glue
Sit on my round kindergarten table
And make a heart for you
I knew you didn't have one
I wanted to make you care
No glue stick
Can make you stuck to anyone
How childish
I don't do arts and crafts anymore

WHERE WILDFLOWERS BLOOM

You were about to eat my heart out
I was the one setting the table
Handing over the fork
With a napkin

I gave you the knife
That you cut me open with

I gave you the power
To rip me apart

AYANA FAROOQ

I lay awake
When the night sky is the colour of overripe mulberries

Worries pop into my mind
Like jealous green leaves sprouting on the fruit tree

The one in the family garden
That's been watered by all those tears

The one that wears its branches
Like wolvish claws
And its imposing figure casts the world in its shade

Every generation sows its seeds
Ones that seem manageable now

Then become thorny and overgrown later on

The garden was rife with the fruits of life
Hanging low
All falling closely to the tree

We used to stare at them longingly as children
Hoping to get a burst of pleasure
Out of the endless suffering

And now the air smells of pungent wine
Flies feast on all the sweet things we left to rot

WHERE WILDFLOWERS BLOOM

Flames danced in your pupils
You shot torched arrow after arrow
Setting the forest ablaze

You said this was how civilization was built
You said you could make me into something
I needed to become soft and moldable first
Weak

You needed to shape my thoughts
The fire was needed to forge me into your weapon

AYANA FAROOQ

You only live in the steps of joyful people
Rampant at basketball games
VIP concerts
But as soon as I am down
And need to spring back up
You bounce
Knocking me to my knees
Dazzling the entire school
Hypnotized by your movements
You hug them tightly
Like a friend
You sap all their energy
And then get restless bored
Bouncing on to the next and the next and next
And you circle back to hurt me more
Your jump infiltrates my hands
Your cruel snicker bounces in my head
Your essence lives in my words
I hope they will dance in your mind a little
To rattle you enough
So you stay put
And now I have got to bounce

WHERE WILDFLOWERS BLOOM

You were like the bundle of roses you handed to me
Your words sweet as nectar
Your smile gleaming white
Like those petals

But as soon as I held you tightly
When it was too late to see what was underneath

Your thorns pierced me

PREY

WHERE WILDFLOWERS BLOOM

Why are good and bad things so similar
I always confuse salt with sugar
Fire and frost both burn me
Maybe that's why I can never tell the difference
Between those that love and loathe me

AYANA FAROOQ

Not everything shows up on the X-ray
I'm in fragments
My spirit ripped to shreds
But I'm whole
On the black and white picture of the X-ray

WHERE WILDFLOWERS BLOOM

When real life starts to crumble
We play makeup
Splatter the world in glitter
We coat things that are decaying
Make clouds of blush
Figurines of mascara
Castles of lip gloss
It's easy to get lost in
Painting over your identity
Forgetting who you are

AYANA FAROOQ

I form a fist around
A rose
Dipped in morning dew
The colour of blackberry juice
Sprinkled with fresh raindrops
That glisten like tears
I try to crush it
Try to destroy
The love I have for you
But that only
Imprints your sweet perfumed scent
Further into my mind

WHERE WILDFLOWERS BLOOM

Cruel Ebony hands
Taking time away
They never stop grabbing my life from me
They never stop ticking
It's round face mocking me
Reminding me that I'm mortal
Making me restless
I can't sit still
The hour hand starts to carve wrinkles
The minute hand inflicts pain in my joints
The second hand paints my hair gray
My hand must fill every moment with production

AYANA FAROOQ

My ocean skin glistened
My forests vibrant and youthful
I watched you grow up
Watched you crawl around on all fours
Watched you swing and jump on the playgrounds I built

I was peppered with a slight cough
Some burnt coal and cinders had found their way into my lungs
It was nothing serious though
I could not be prouder
Of the great castles and marvelous boats
Of everything you achieved and accomplished

My ocean skin is blemished with plastic
My forests have been reduced to ash
I have heat spikes and flashes
I'm trapped in greenhouse gasses
Choked for breath
On my deathbed
It's time for you to take care of me now

WHERE WILDFLOWERS BLOOM

I was waxen
Pale and plain
Weak from disappointment
Yet another night
Where the earth didn't glance my way
It only looked at the raging sun
Its flash and magnificence
I was always there
Shining light when the nights were inky black

But we never notice those who revolve around us

AYANA FAROOQ

The once nimble fingered factory worker
Stood before her supervisor
Old and shrivelled

Like an orange
When it's flesh and juice is sucked away
And all that remains is the peel

She begged him
She gave him all her juice
Her essence

When she was young

But he chucked her
Into the garbage filled streets

As easily as tossing an orange peel
In the trash
After you've finished with the fruit

WHERE WILDFLOWERS BLOOM

You were like a meek and fragile leaf
Letting the wind determine where you land in life
The predators of the forest trance all over you
You get torn up so easily
Not strong enough to make ripples in the water
You have no power
No control
Unable to take a step

You are a cushion for the mighty and powerful
When they tumble
You are there
Springing them back up
Without a scratch
Where you are crushed
And buried
Deep within the earth
Where nobody can see you

AYANA FAROOQ

I jump into your leather embrace
When there is no one else to turn to
You are a great listener
I spill my inky black heart
Onto your blank face
Where you don't judge me
Where you won't notice when my tears fall and obscure you
Where you won't notice my face contorted in anguish
You sit there silently
Absorbing all my pain

WHERE WILDFLOWERS BLOOM

Rust coats my pencil
It used to be a fountain
From which words sprung
It's pipes no longer run smoothly
The fountain is not a sight of beauty
Uneven spurts erupt
Instead of cool precise crystalline water
I think the problem started with the pump
With my heart
It got broken
Stabbed over and over
Until it's wounds became infected
Diseased
Then spread
Through the passages of blood
To my fingertips
To my cherished pencil
I tried to fix it
To shake off the rusted machinery
But this isn't a cure
I've only spread it further
And now this poem is
Tarnished

AYANA FAROOQ

Sometimes I want to forget everything and go to the reef
Where the ocean is cool and the air is warm
Where coral paints a pretty picture for me
Where teems of silver minnows
Bathe me in glitter
Where you can dive deep under
And feel weightless
Where you can't hear a sound
Where time freezes too
I could get lost in there
Live in a bubble
It takes everything to get out
Freezing dripping wet
Awakened to the sharp pain of reality

WHERE WILDFLOWERS BLOOM

I had a heart of glass

One that was curved to magnify
So people could see my every emotion

One that was a poor reflection of the things around it
The things it tried so hard to be

One that tried to lie to me
Refract and distort things

Create a false world
That I'd be happier with

One that looked so much like ice from afar

But it shatters into a million pieces
With one knock from you

AYANA FAROOQ

I was a chameleon
Flitting back and forth
Morphing so my scales looked like the silver coats of wolves
Or the russet of oak trees
One day I was firm and stoic like a boulder
And the next I flowed easily like a river
I didn't know who I was
I spent my days waiting
For my true colours to show

WHERE WILDFLOWERS BLOOM

I'm wilted in a field of lavenders
All the other flowers are ramrod straight

They were farmed that way

They are crushed into perfume
Masking rotten things of this world
But not fixing them

They bloom in all their purple glory

Sweet nectar
Trying to cover poisonous pesticides

They are picked up
Run dry
And objectified
Drained of their essence
So they can decorate the world
Instead of making it better

They stand in rows
Like kids at school
Houses in the suburbs

And block out the sun
From the wildflowers

AYANA FAROOQ

Everything is grey
But pulses of gold

Cool metallic silver
The colour of storm clouds
You drown under
Of gravestones
Where you bury yourself
Of the chains
That trap your happiness

All for a shade
All for a moment

Where your veins flood with sunlight
Tears fall like deep yellow leaves in autumn
Your eyes sparkle with amber
You grab for cheap polyester fabric
Strung around a poorly gilded circle of metal
You pile another leaden burden on your shoulders

WHERE WILDFLOWERS BLOOM

I used to be natural
In my childhood
Chattering with the ease of a fast flowing river
Dancing like reeds in the wind
I'd beam for the whole world to see
Just like the radiant sun
At dawn
I had so much hope
Now I'm mechanical
Machine-like
My body awkwardly jolts forward
Commanded
By your remote control

The black leaves rose high into the sky
This autumn

Tall willows
Biked off into the moonset

Glittering birds swam and twirled
In the deep pink ocean

Furry fish flew
Across bright green skies

Strawberries didn't rot
People were perfect

In this world
Just maybe
You and I could be together

WHERE WILDFLOWERS BLOOM

Tomorrow I will rest my weary body
Extend my limbs on a sturdy lounge chair
Bask in the golden sun
Tomorrow my tension will evaporate
With the salted ocean
Worries washed with waves
Tomorrow I will feel the touch of grainy sand
Tomorrow I will take the time to peel through the pages
Of a leather bound book
Tomorrow I'll be happy

THE GROUNDS

WHERE WILDFLOWERS BLOOM

Back then I thought the sturdy boulders
Lining the border of the lake
Formed a castle
Not a prison
During springtime they were softened by spongy mosses
That helped you form footholds
So you could climb out
Let your legs dangle off the cliffside
And see the sun's majestic reflection against the water

AYANA FAROOQ

Algae glittered
Green jewels in a serene lake
They were utterly free
With no bones forcing them to be structured
To be in rigid routines and formations
Weightless
Where it can't hear the world's relentless noise
Where the current wipes everything of substance away
It's unburdened by thought
It's just there
Happily anchored still
Watching the world move by it

WHERE WILDFLOWERS BLOOM

Basket of life
Held by wooden arms of maple
Woven without any sharp bits sticking out
With layers thick and soft
To trap heat
To block all of the noise outside
The clumps of twigs forming a nest
Look like clusters of trees in a forest
Their speckled eggs kept in darkness of everything around them
In the forest all I see is the sky
And the trees woven around me
And a sun full of hope

There was an outline of wet sand
Encasing the fast flowing river
The sand was warm
Had that comforting grainy texture
A safe place to bury treasure
There were troves of crayfish
Brown and rusted like wood chests
There were iridescent mussel shells
That shone like golden coins
I thought that I had as much wealth as kings
I never yearned for more

WHERE WILDFLOWERS BLOOM

The looping of O's Curves of C's
They form lapping ocean waves

Their sound raw and unfiltered
Bringing me into a state of tranquil relaxation

Strong and steady
Unfaltering

My pen etches an ocean
While my mouth only utters a quiet stream
Filled with jagged rocks blocking it's flow

I pepper words
Sprinkling tiny grains of sand
Until they make a warm beach

I spew stanzas
With bright passion
Trying to make them shine
Like a raging sun

Every time my pen touches paper
It creates a portal to my paradise

AYANA FAROOQ

I had a wild imagination
A circle of flowers
Tied together by my clumsy hands
I placed it over my head
I thought that it made me an empress
That I had control of the forest
Of what paths it opened for me
Whenever the wind roared It was a knight swiftly sweeping me away
A gnarly tree was a charming castle spire
I could turn writhing salmon
Into glistening mermaids
I could turn a forest into a fairytale

WHERE WILDFLOWERS BLOOM

The sun was young
Not fully emerged
Peeking over at me
It's yolk cracked open over the limitless sky
Dribbling a stream of majestic colors
Thrumming with energy
With anticipation
A rising star
Ready to light up this new world

AYANA FAROOQ

There was a mist
Sprinkled on the tops of mountains
Suspended over the lake and it's turquoise glimmer

It had beauty
Glittered like sugar
And tasted sweet
Innocent

It was like a tiara
Draping the forest
Blocking out the sun's harsh illumination
Cultivating the perfect weather

I wish
I could remove it
As I sat on a bolder
Looking at the lake

Just for an instant
For a glimpse
At what lies beyond

WHERE WILDFLOWERS BLOOM

The green leaves were vibrant
Nothing looked dead or stale
All the colours looked like a fresh set of children's markers
Sprinkles of buttercups
Of wild roses
Lavenders
The world was a blank canvas
You could draw anything
Be anything
The markers had not run dry
The ink had not been seeped from the earth

AYANA FAROOQ

The clouds looked so distant back then
They looked like tufts of cotton candy
With a coppery shine
From the sun's rays
They glided slowly
Their gradual trek towards me
Was almost too slight to notice
But I spent a lot of time with my head up in those clouds
I would dance with them
As they twirled with fluffy ball gowns
Spinning and spinning
Getting closer and closer
To covering the heart of the sunrise

THE HUNT

AYANA FAROOQ

You came without warning
I watched helplessly
As you rowed with well muscled arms
Your boat of ash and cinders
As you approached the sun peaked
The mist parted
The flowers died
The leaves fell
My bloodshot eyes squinted
At your graceful figure
At your bow slung around your cold shoulder
And your arrows of fire aimed my way
I felt my scaled chameleon skin shifting
Turning into a deer's hide
And I felt a frosty breeze chill my bones
An archers breath down my neck
And so the hunt began

WHERE WILDFLOWERS BLOOM

You only love me for my form
Thin as paper
My body brushed with swirls of black ink
We're told to be easy to digest
So you're able to devour us over and over
But you can't glimpse the thorns beneath
My flowery speech
Can't see that underneath my plain fragile exterior
I hold oceans of wisdom and meaning
That I have the strength to endure eons
I'm a poem
Lingering elegantly on your lips
Until I pierce your heart
And you dare tell me
That I'm only valuable
If I can catch your wandering eye

AYANA FAROOQ

I grew up on a farm
Not the charming kind
With rolling hills
Where golden bits of straw gleamed in your hair
Still there were farmers
Amongst the tall glass skyscrapers
They'd start by throwing away the bad seeds
Chucking them in sandy soil
Not giving them water, attention or nourishment
Leaving them for dead
For those of us lucky enough to be on fertile soil
We were fed pesticides of ideology
Taught to kill insects because they were different from us
Our DNA was altered
They tried to suppress our identities
Our imperfections
So we'd be more useful for them
And then after years of striving for their approval
As soon as we begun to wrinkle
They sucked our juice
Devoured us whole
Until all that remained of us
Was a sour taste on their lips

WHERE WILDFLOWERS BLOOM

A robin cocooned in liquid
In a protective shell
I'm buried in emotions
I form walls to block the world outside

It weakly cracks it's egg open
My heart begins to thaw

It's eyes open to the world
I'm able to see beauty

Weak but alive
I'm fragile but living

The bird takes flight
And my spirits launch with it

AYANA FAROOQ

You took over all the best parts
You sat there like a conquering emperor
Basked on the golden beach
Hoarded the iridescent muscles
You ate all the sweet berries
You stole the honeycombs
You took away everything that brought a smile to my face

WHERE WILDFLOWERS BLOOM

Through the seams of fabric
The bars of my cage
I glimpse the garden

The flowers look like silk

Their roots digging into the soil

Like threads embroidered
In a leaden veil

Golden leaves
Pale flecks of gold
Littered across barren ground
If I look closely there's an even pattern
Those jagged diamond squares
The ones across my gown

The soil
Looks magical
And rich as dark obsidian gems
The backdrop of my dress

It looks airy, fluffy

Light and beautiful

But it suffocates
The earth's molten fiery core
It's taking away the air from my lungs
Squeezing out all the passion in my soul

I am not a quiet garden

AYANA FAROOQ

The earth's depth extends far below
It's delicate surface

A tiny frilly layer of crust
Like the dress sown into my skin

I am fire and power
A volcano
That is erupting
I will burn the garment– the bonnet, the hijab, the prison
From my torso

WHERE WILDFLOWERS BLOOM

Broomsticks
Were shoved into our hands
We slaved around houses
Cleaning up your filthy footprints
Your muddy morals
Paved the way to success
Swept away all your worries
And got nothing but tufts of dirt in our faces
We managed to soar
With the only objects we were given
And then we were branded witches

AYANA FAROOQ

The salted ocean breeze
Peppermint and hibiscus perfume
The gold sun peaking through leafy canopies
Fresh river currents brushing my skin
Rocky paths with green moss
Tiny creatures hidden inside small blades of grass

The smell of rotting fish
The grimy dirt covering plants
The blinding sun searing my eyes
The river making me cold
The bugs invading the grass

It's these choices that determine the life we live

WHERE WILDFLOWERS BLOOM

I was put in a box
When I was 3

It was glued shut
With the paste of repetition

Every uniformed word I wrote in essays
Etched me deeper into a bottomless abyss

The box was dark
No light of ingenuity
No glimmer of illumination

It squished you into a square
Stunting my growth

No space for individuality

It hurt my head
To break out of the warm cardboard

I tasted the sweet crisp air and fully extended my limbs
And wondered why be a square
When we were born shaped like stars

AYANA FAROOQ

I feel like a piece of flotsam
Being beaten on by waves
Having no power over where I land
Letting powerful currents determine my path
You eroded my splinters of personality
Molded me closer to your shape
I was cold and dark and seasick
With a flick of luck I found a sandy oasis
One where there were other pieces like me
Where together we became whole
Our ship was no longer broken
And we could steer it in any direction we choose

WHERE WILDFLOWERS BLOOM

I never knew the difference between a butterfly and a moth
I saw the same steady flutter
As they came to land on my ticklish nose
They both spread hope and pollen
The only difference I saw was the name
But a name could not change
The rising feeling in your chest
As you watched a tiny moth
Beat its beautifully crafted wings
It didn't change
The way their white specks glitter like pearls
And their swirly patterns look like impressionist paintings
It doesn't change
The way they unfurl their safe cocoons
And leap without hesitation into the crisp spring air

AYANA FAROOQ

My callused fingers
Coated in specks of cerulean blue
Chips of magenta, canary yellow

Struggled to capture your essence

In my torn notebook
I traced the outline of your collarbone
Drew you close to me

Sketched and sketched
Knowing that I'll only get to touch you
If you're made of ink

I brushed your lips
With the most striking of reds
It didn't capture your vibrant smile

The whites of my canvas
Didn't twinkle like the stars in your eyes

I hoped if I scratched you out in ink and oils
You would stop living in my mind

WHERE WILDFLOWERS BLOOM

I saw garden snakes
They slithered like bolts of lightning
With black and yellow stripes
Spring was when they were sleek and shiny
When they shed off all of their old cruelty
Left behind leathers of lies and deceit
If they could choose to turn good
I thought there was hope for everyone
I didn't realize human skin didn't shed so easily

AYANA FAROOQ

I palmed your heart
While trying to pilfer scraps from your grave

It stuck to my hand
Like the bunches of sticky rice you'd make every Saturday

It was deformed
A little sickly

And somehow you made room for the entire world there

Maybe it malfunctioned
Because there were too many chunks of gold inside

I felt like I had to be a thief whenever
I tiptoed around your memory
I wanted to steal bits and pieces of your character from death
Make them a part of me

I snuck off into the night
With your precious golden heart
Willing it to work again

But it never did

You imbued bits in pieces into me, my siblings
And everyone you touched on earth

WHERE WILDFLOWERS BLOOM

The garden of butterflies
A much needed sight for my wary eyes

Until they form tears
Sprinkling onto the pale green aloe vera

Dew drops like melted sugar

If only the bile rising in my mouth was so sweet

Sweet like how you tenderly planted

Those soft wildflowers
With petals that glistened like your eyes
And roots that led back to you

But never lived to see them bloom

WHERE WILDFLOWERS BLOOM

www.ingramcontent.com/pod-product-compliance
Lightning Source LLC
Chambersburg PA
CBHW050330010526
44119CB00050B/741